HOLLY ALEXANDER

ADVANCED

MAGIC MONEY

A COURSE IN

CREATING

ABUNDANCE

BOOK TWO

HOLLY ALEXANDER

ADVANCED

MAGIC
MONEY

*A COURSE IN CREATING
ABUNDANCE*

BOOK TWO

Published by Magic Money Books

Print ISBN: 978-1-947665-75-0
Digital ISBN: 978-1-947665-99-6

YOU'RE INVITED

would like to personally invite you to the Magic Money Books community at Facebook.com/groups/MagicMoneyBooks where you can join in on the magic! You'll find daily support, affirmations, and inspiration from like-minded individuals on their own magic money journey.

I'd also love to hear from you personally! You can connect with me through email at Holly@MagicMoneyBooks.com. I look forward to connecting and hearing about your magic money journey soon!

TABLE OF CONTENTS

Chapter One:

Advanced Magic Money 1

Chapter Two:

Preparing for Your Second
Magic Money Experiment:
Setting Your Intention 9

Chapter Three:

Setting Your Intention *in Writing* 23

Chapter Four:

Setting Your Intention
with Visualization 47

Chapter Five:

Setting Your Intention
through Your Words 57

Chapter Six:

More Magic Money Maximization 85

Chapter Seven:

Your Second Magic
Money Experiment 105

Chapter Eight:

More Magic Money Mastery 115

Gratitude 121

Who is Holly 122

Dear Reader,

Welcome to *Advanced Magic Money*, the second in a three-book series. If you've stumbled upon this book before reading *Beginning Magic Money*, you'll want to start there (trust me on this one).

Advanced Magic Money was written to help you continue to take tiny yet incredibly important steps toward a life of abundance of money and anything and everything else your heart desires.

If you have been committed to your Magic Money practice for thirty days or more, you no doubt have a strong foundation for what's next: maximizing your money through your actions and taking your mindset up several notches.

Imagine being in a place where you always know you have more than enough money in your spending account, in your savings account, in other reserve and investment accounts, and on its way to you. In other words, you can reach a level of financial abundance that until today you thought was impossible.

But lest you think I've lost my mind and am abandoning my commitment to practicality, that is the furthest thing from reality!

Expanding your consciousness happens one thought and one action at a time, consistently executed over an initial period to get it going, and for the rest of your life. After all, you don't want to live in a world of magic money for a finite period, right? I know, me either.

Let's begin.

Holly Alexander

Chapter One

ADVANCED MAGIC MONEY

Magic Money is the wonderful abundance
(including money) you attract into your life in
expected and unexpected ways through the practice
of the Magic Money Philosophy.

The Magic Money Philosophy can be
summed up in these twenty-seven words:

*Focus the endless energy of your mind on abundance,
and treat all you receive with respect, and you will
have unlimited abundance—because of, or despite,
what is happening around you.*

It is through writing, visualization, and speaking prosperous words, you can not only eliminate any remaining limiting beliefs you hold, but you can also finally, and permanently, allow the massive abundance that is yours by divine right into your life.

It is a bold statement, I know, and not one I make lightly. I say these words with complete confidence because I am living proof that no matter what you come from, or how much you have had to struggle, a life of magic, miracles, and abundance is possible—and it can happen easier and sooner than you think!

I never, in a million years, thought I would share my Magic Money Philosophy with anyone, let alone write not one, but three books, on the subject. Over the years, I have shared the Magic Money Philosophy with a select group of people, you'll know them as the Experimenters in *Beginning Magic Money*. The only reason I shared what I was doing with them is that they were close enough to me to see what was happening in my life and they were curious. *How did you do that?* they would ask, knowing I did not come from money, so I didn't have a "rich dad" to plump up my bank account. *That's incredible!* they would exclaim when I would receive the exact thing or

2

amount of money I would ask for, sometimes within moments of setting my intention (which usually came in the form of a simple *It would be great if 'x' would happen...* statement).

Eventually, I had to come clean and share with them the practical and prosperity processes I was using, and they too stepped into the flow of magic money and unlimited abundance in all ways.

The same is possible for you, especially if you've completed your first magic money experiment. By spending 30, 60, or 90 days grabbing ahold of your thoughts and words, you've set the stage to move to the next level of the Magic Money Philosophy. I'm excited for you because I know what's possible and about to happen in your life. I'm trying to contain myself as I write this ... **smile**.

With a genuine commitment on your part and a tiny bit of faith in the Magic Money Philosophy, you can drastically shift the results in your life. Having an abundance of money *is just the beginning*. The Magic Money Philosophy allows for an abundance of anything and everything your heart desires. It will take work on your part, but from where I sit, the "work" isn't work at all! It is a massive amount of fun.

The experiments are delightful to engage in, and they produce exciting and surprisingly wonderful results. As you play around with the strategies and ideas in these books, you'll live in a constant state of astonishment and wonder as money flows into your life, and you receive unexpected gifts, checks, refunds, discounts, favors, and special treatment.

For your part, you will participate with as much commitment and gusto as you can muster, and here's how:

To fully and successfully participate in the Magic Money Philosophy, decide right now you're going to:

- Take control of what you think, say, and do with money, **and**

- suspend any disbelief you are holding in reserve; **and**

- let go of every belief that money must come to you through specific channels (i.e., through your job/career); **and**

- think and speak about money in a positive way; **and**

- allow money to come to you from anywhere at any time; **and**

4

- believe that there's more than enough for you now and henceforth forever, **and**

- expect an abundance of everything you need is indeed on it's way to you *right now*.

Isn't is time for you to be open to receive all that you want out of life, including money and an abundance of anything and everything you want and need? I think so!

Above is the mindset side of the Magic Money Philosophy. There is also the practical action side of the Magic Money Philosophy. You must also decide right now to:

- be respectful toward your money at all times, **and**

- spend your money with intention and purpose, **and**

- save your money with intention and purpose, **and**

- have fun with your money on purpose, **and**

- grow your money with intention and purpose.

We're going to start with the mental side of the Magic Money Philosophy first, then dive into the actions you must take to put, and keep, yourself in the continuous flow of money. Just to let you in on something cool, let me say this: once you start and begin to see results, you won't be able to do your Magic Money Philosophy actions fast enough. I promise you will not only have the time of your life playing with the Magic Money Philosophy. You'll get addicted (in the best possible way) to the results you get and want to use them every day, in every way.

On that note, you might be wondering if you should continue the actions of your First Magic Money Experiment. The answer is: *absolutely*. You wouldn't want to "break the magic" by going back to your old ways of being, right?

You must continue to:

One. **Take responsibility for your life and everything in it.**

If anything happens you don't like, remember (and recite) your Statement of Responsibility: *I take full responsibility for my life and everything in it.*

6

Two. **No complaining, bemoaning, or bellyaching.**

No more criticizing. Not even a tiny bit of gossiping, back-fence talking, or scuttlebutt discussing. Your mantra is: *Everything is working out for my highest good, and I can't wait to see what happens next!*

Three. **Keep adding to your gratitude list daily and if you're feeling less-than-abundant, review the list from day one!**

Remember the Magic Money Accelerator: Thank you notes!

Four. **You receive, make, or find money and add it to your list.**

In other words, the above four practices can only serve you if you do them. *And, there's so much more to come.*

Are you in? If so, let's go!

Chapter Two

PREPARING FOR YOUR SECOND MAGIC MONEY EXPERIMENT:

Setting Your Intention

The creator of the rich universe we inhabit has provided abundance—an abundance of everything we could ever possibly want or use, and which, in fact, is available to us. It is up to us to take the invisible and turn it into the visible. We can take our ideas, desires, and opportunities and shape and form them through our thoughts, words, and actions.

9

A simple concept, for sure, but not always easy, at least at first. You might have spent the better part of your life living in fear that you wouldn't have enough, or angry that other people always seem to have more than you. Ultimately, however, you and you alone inform and influence your financial state, and *you and you alone* get to decide how wealthy you want to be.

It is a good day when you realize you are the master of this universe, your universe! Which also really does make you master of your destiny and your abundance. In *Beginning Magic Money*, I gave you a peek into what a life of abundance could mean, and the first steps for how to create it for yourself.

Hopefully, by the time you read this, you have completed thirty days (or more) of your first Magic Money experiment, and your Magic Money Mindset is expanding day by day as you take note of all of the magic money and other miracles that come into your life. You might not fully believe everything I say, but you are cautiously optimistic (or, you're completely on board and can't wait for what's next).

But wait, there's more!

You've picked what was behind "Door Number 1" when you began your first experiment. You're in for more because you're here, which tells me you either secretly or not-so-secretly want more. I'm excited for you because your first experiment revealed just a tiny glimpse of what is possible! You now have an idea how powerful and magical you are.

By continuing to engage in the Magic Money Philosophy, you get access to what's behind *all of the doors*. An unlimited amount of money and an abundance of anything else you could want is truly available to you. And gaining access to it isn't hard, doesn't require backbreaking work or super-human skills. As I've said, an abundance of everything you want is easier and closer than you can imagine.

You take absolute control of, and unleash, your abundance deliberately with your thoughts, words, and actions. You first 30-Day Experiment in *Beginning Magic Money* may have been the very first time you thought about money and abundance in this way. You intentionally focused solely on the positive, and purposefully directed your mind to think and speak only on goodness and abundance. I can promise you it was truly only the beginning. Your Magic Money Journal

11

probably has quite a list of the goodness that showed up during your experiment. Eventually there will be so much evidence of abundance; such an overwhelming amount of *magic money*. At some point, you will only take note of the top five things to happen every day. If you wrote all the magic money happenings down, that is all you would do!

In doing the experiment for yourself, you might have had a light bulb moment (or many) along the lines of:

- When I focus on good things, good things happen.

- When I notice and record money that comes to me, more and more money comes to me.

- *There really is an abundance of everything available to me.* (My personal favorite.)

You now know there is truly an abundance: all around you and available to you. Perhaps you've even had the realization it was there all along, but you weren't focusing on it or didn't quite believe it. But now that you are tuned in, you recognize all you need (including, but not limited to, money) is on the other side of your thoughts. Said a bit differently, when you focus on plenty, you have plenty.

Once you have realized there is plenty available to you, you might be wondering what must happen for you to have more, get more, manifest more.

I wondered the same thing, and I've got you covered, for sure!

Remember in *Beginning Magic Money* when I talked about maximizing your money? And you probably scrunched up your nose a little with confusion when I gave you that first experiment and there was nothing you were supposed to do differently with your money.

I chose to do that for two reasons:

One. Beliefs often follow results.

To begin to believe there is more than enough money *for you*, you would have to get, and remain, in the place of a permanent belief. To install that one belief, you had to have one sole focus: to find evidence of abundance and record it. Simultaneously, you had to give up any verbal practices you might have (ahem) that didn't serve you.

13

Two. **There is something to be said for not expecting or trying to do too much too soon.**

To fully own your new state of being, you had to experience gradual and incremental changes. Practice doesn't make perfect; *practice makes permanent.*

What You Want Can Come to You in Magical Ways, At the Perfect Time, In an Easy Way

Any intention you set for yourself might not manifest through money you receive. In fact, although these books seemingly are just about "magic money" they could be retitled to "magic everything." The truth is your desired good can and will come to you through literally millions of channels.

You don't have to have money to get what you want. Just as money can come to you through unlimited channels, so can your desires.

Most of us have been taught (or programmed) to think money comes through hard work (usually from a job). Here's the truth: money can come from anywhere! Money continues to come

14

through new and interesting and magical ways to my fellow Experimenters and me all the time! The thing for you to keep in mind is that when you ask for something, *your part is complete.* When you place an order online, do you care if it comes in the mail, or through FEDEX, or DHL, or UPS? Or through a major freight company? Or even a private delivery service? I don't if I get exactly what I ordered. My advice is to keep your mind open, and never underestimate the Universe!

Timing is Everything

When I decide I want something, I usually want it *now.* I'm often asked when I want or need something by one of my team members, and my answer is always, *Why yesterday, of course!* However, I have learned is two-fold: what I want always shows up in a magical way, and always, *always* in its own timing. I have had something *huge* on my list for a couple of years now. My husband and I have done lots of preparation for it, talked about it, and put it on our lists. We have even practiced the money management strategies I talked about in *Beginning Magic Money* and expand upon in this book. The timing hasn't been exactly perfect, and so we are still waiting.

We are waiting with positive expectation because we know it is coming, it's a sure thing. We just simply don't know what day to circle in red on our calendars, and we're okay with that!

Why? Because the Universe is on its own timing. It seems to have a wonderful way of sorting things out. Here's the coolest part:

- What I ask for always shows up.

- It is either exactly what I asked for, or...

- It is so much better I'm left with a huge smile on my face and shaking my head at the unbelievable-ness of it all.

I often say to this magical Universe, *Now you're just showing off!*

If you're in the beginning stages of the Magic Money Philosophy and what you need is gas money, I have two things to say:

1. Go back and do another thirty days of Your First Money Experiment.

2. Magic Money can and will show up at the perfect moment, even if it is exactly the very last minute you need it and your heart is beating out of your chest.

I've received checks as I'm pulling out of town on vacation, see the mail truck and grab my mail. I've gone to bed thinking, *It would be great to have an additional $500 to pay for that insurance,* only to wake up to an email notification I received monies owed to me from a long-forgotten venture, refund, bonus, or even a gift! Sometimes it is exactly the amount needed, and sometimes it is many multiples.

Being Unattached.

Becoming unattached to the "how, how much and when" is a skill. Like any skill, it is developed through trial and error, otherwise known as practice. When you set an intention by writing it down, visualizing it, or using your words, you're throwing the full weight of your desire behind it. But ultimately, you're going to get the best results if you can say *It would be cool if this happens* and then let it go. Whether it happens or not, you're all good. It doesn't matter if it happens or not, because you know the Universe is conspiring on your behalf to deliver to you everything you could want, and more, and better.

Your Second Magic Money Experiment

Hopefully, you haven't jumped into *Advanced Magic Money* without a solid thirty or more days of your first experiment. But if you have, I don't blame you. I am the type of person who would read all three books, and then begin again at the beginning. (Just be sure to do at least thirty days of the First Magic Money Experiment before you take on the more advanced strategies of this book and in *Magic Money Mastery,* okay? Okay!)

Regardless, you're here, and I'm going to assume you've completed at least thirty days of the first experiment. Which means it's time to expand your consciousness by learning more about the Magic Money Philosophy and engaging in your Second Magic Money Experiment.

Just as the Magic Money Philosophy has both a prosperity and practical side to it, your Second Magic Money Experiment has multiple aspects, starting with *Setting Your Intention.*

Setting Your Intention

Here you are, ready to begin your Second Magic Money Experiment, somewhere between cautiously optimistic and gleeful. Beyond a shadow of a doubt, if you have been looking out for money everywhere I *know* you've been finding it. No, I don't have a crystal ball or a hidden camera in your kitchen. I just know it because it works. It's worked for me and countless others, some of whom you have read about in the first book.

Your Second Magic Money Experiment is going to eliminate all remaining doubt and eradicate any limiting beliefs you hold and help you embrace the *fact* that you are connected to an unending stream of magic money and unlimited abundance. If you are chalking up the past month or two (or three) to beginner's luck or chance, it's time to remove, once and for all, any doubt that remains. Let's replace it with the fact that you and you alone can manifest what you need, and eliminate the worry and fear you've had about money.

In the previous experiment, your sole focus was on your thoughts and words. Again, I didn't ask you to change how you handled your money.

This is because it's imperative that you get your mind into the right space first before attempting to change behavior and taking different actions. Now you're ready to experience the added benefit of changing a bit of what you do, in addition to changing how you think and speak.

As in the first experiment, you are about to set an intention. Only this time the intention you set is for something you want. Not only that, it is for something you want, yet at precisely this moment you have absolutely no idea how it could happen. You don't have even the first thought about how you're going to get the money to pay for it or how it might show up for you.

By now, your intention setting muscles might be relatively strong. You may just think *I'm going to be thrilled when I board the plane to Paris for the first time*, or *I'm going to love driving my new Infiniti QX80*. And then get on with your day, knowing what you've intended is going to show up.

This intention might still feel just beyond, or even way beyond, what you're capable of at this stage of the game. To that end, there are three powerful ways I've used in the past (and still sometimes use) you can use to communicate your intended desire to the Universe.

Here is the first step in your Second Magic Money Experiment:

Identify something you want. Make it something so amazing, so big, that you simply can't see a way it could ever happen! This is so that when it happens, you'll know it is the ultimate sign that the Magic Money Philosophy works, that YOU are as magical and powerful as I'm telling you that you are.

There are several ways of setting an intention, and one of them is a passing thought, similar to what I said above … *It would be great if this or that were to happen.*

But I know you're most likely still new to this process, and if I were you (and I once was, I promise), I would want practical, tangible action steps I could take that also work. Fair enough. I'm with you on this one. In the coming three chapters, I share three tried-and-true ways to set an intention, with a couple of options contained within each one.

Go ahead and decide what you want your next intention to be, then read these three next chapters. I'll continue this part of our conversation soon!

Chapter Three

SETTING YOUR INTENTION *IN WRITING*

In your First Magic Money Experiment, you set an intention to manifest something specific. You may have noticed I asked you to write it down. In fact, there was a lot of "write that down" in your Experiment. By the end of this chapter, you'll understand why *in writing* is, and was, so important.

There are three key ways to set an intention: *in writing, through visualization,* and *through speaking.*

All three ways of setting your intention work like a charm, I promise. You will benefit from knowing multiple ways to set intentions. Ultimately, you will find which ones work the best for you.

Quick! Pull out your Magic Money Journal and perhaps some different colored pens or markers. You're going to need them!

In Writing

The first way to set your intention, which you have already used, is *in writing*. Writing down your desires is tangible—your desire is transferred from something you "only" see in your mind to something you can read on paper (or wherever you write it).

Notes from the Universe

Mike Dooley, the author of *Thoughts are Things*, is famous for his "Notes from the Universe." This method of setting your intention is to send a Note *to* the Universe.

Get a sheet of stationary or nice piece of paper and a pen, or if you prefer, use your computer, to draft a letter stating your desires. Find a place where you won't be disturbed until

24

you're finished (put your phone on airplane mode, turn off any computer notifications, and put a sign on your office door).

Begin *Dear Universe, It is so amazing that* … and describe what you desire as though you're already experiencing it, you already have it. Describe what it's like, now that you're with the love of your life, living an abundant life, or driving your brand-new car.

Put yourself fully into what you desire to experience or receive as if you're experiencing it now. I mean, if you wrote down, *It is so amazing I got the $85,000 I needed to buy my new Audi! OMG, it is so fun to drive! I love how the dashboard lights up at night, and how fast I can go on the freeway! The State Highway Patrol will never catch me now! LOL!*

How would you feel if FEDEX knocked on the door and delivered the check right now? Pretty amazing, right? You would do the Snoopy dance! You would be in the end zone getting a major fine from the League office for "inappropriate celebration!" *And you'd be too happy and excited to care about anything else!*

Think about the last time you said or thought that nothing could bring you down, you were so excited. Channel *that guy!* That is the exact state you need to be in when you write your note.

Write all of those "so excited you can hardly stand it right now" thoughts and emotions in your *Note.*

Need another way? I've got you covered. Remember the last time something amazing happened to you? You picked up the phone and called your best friend or your mom and told them all about it. They might even have said, *Slow down! You're talking so fast I can't understand you!* You described what led up to the awesomeness, and then every detail of the event.

You're going to do that again. Only this time you imagine how delightful your manifestation is going to be as though it has just happened. This time, get as excited as if it had already happened, and write about it in the "just past" tense (i.e., it happened two hours ago or yesterday and you're still fired up about it). Your goal is to make it so real you can no longer feel any lack or limitation. You only feel incredible joy and excitement about the fact that what you've wanted has finally come to you. You're thrilled. You're grateful. Right now.

Every time you think about the intention you've set, say to yourself (silently or aloud), *It is so amazing that ...* (fill in the blank). Then say a big thank you to the Universe and get back to doing whatever you were doing.

You can "mail" your Note to the Universe by putting it inside of an envelope you address to the Universe, and placing it in the back of your journal, in a special book on your bookshelf (such as your Bible), or even under your mattress. Most likely, you'll stumble upon your letter at a time in the future when you'll realize everything you wrote in the letter *magically* came to pass in a most wonderful way! Or, if you're like me, you'll put the letters in a box labeled "Manifestations." and when what I've intended has come to pass, I pull out the *Note*, give thanks again, and replace it with a new one.

List Writing

You can also use a mystical technique written about many times before, yet not known or used as widely as it could be: *the magic of list writing*.

Note: List Writing is not only for your Second Magic Money Experiment. You'll want to use it the rest of your life, every day. I promise you're going to love working with the List Making practice!

First, you must think about what you want. Then, you take outer action by taking your mental pictures and putting them down on paper.

When I first discovered this technique, it seemed simple. Too simple, in fact, that I didn't really think it would work. But! I had practiced tithing and saving, and both had worked to beautifully for me, I decided to give it a try.

I started writing a list every morning of what I wanted to happen each day:

- I engage a new client.

- I'm feeling fantastic today.

- I receive $5,000 in an unexpected and magical way.

- I manifest $36,000 to prepay my rent for a year.

- I engage one new $25,000 client this month.

- I sell $1,000 worth of products today.

Then I'd get on with my day. The following day, I go back and note the ones that had happened. I like to put a smiley face ( ) next to the ones that came to pass, and a smiling face with an exclamation point next to the extra cool stuff (!!). I also double-check my Master List (which I'm going to talk about next), to see which things on the list have come to pass or seem to be coming in the near future.

You can even see how a situation is working out during the day, and write down how you'd like to see it work out. Then, you'll watch with surprise and wonder as it seems to take the shape you've asked for, right before your eyes. But I'm getting a bit ahead of myself ...

Let's start with your Master List, and then we'll discuss the Daily List.

The Master List

Pull out your Magic Money Journal and make a complete list of the things you want in life. Initially, you make one big list, and it can include everything from:

- where you ultimately want to live (could be more than one place!), to

29

- what you want to drive (more than one or even five different cars is an option), to

- a check, signed Contract, or direct deposit you're waiting for,

- a client you want to land, or

- even a trip you want to take.

Remember: the sky is the limit. You are truly limited only to what you and your imagination can cook up.

You can continue to add to this list. And you know what? Over time you're going to revisit the list and put the date each item manifested for you.

Three things that could happen with each item on your list:

1. You receive exactly what you want.

2. You receive something better.

3. You decide you no longer want what's on your list.

Just the act of writing it down sets the Universe in motion to bring about what you want—or something better. I'll be sure and talk about the "other something better" in a minute or two.

But first, I did mention there's another option: sometimes I'll add something to my list and then later decide, upon further reflection, I conclude I do not want it. For example: over time I figured out my original desire: *I want to own and operate a bed and breakfast* wasn't a true desire. I mean, make breakfast for 15-20 people every morning? Wash linens and towels every day? Have strangers constantly in and out of my home? *No thanks!* If something is not your heart's desire, eventually you'll figure it out and cross it off the list. I am positive the Universe also knows the future. It doesn't work hard to bring us the things we think we want now, but will eventually realize we don't want.

Your Master List is a compilation of everything you want. At least once a week, read through it. Confirm with a smile the things you've already written, knowing they are, at that very moment, on their way. While you're at it, if any new desire pops into mind, jot that down, too. Say a little thank you and get on your way. Fun, right? I know, I love my Master List and review and update it often, too.

There's another list practice you'll want to engage in, and this one requires daily attention. There are multiple reasons you'll love this manifesting technique, the main one being the brilliance of its simplicity and effectiveness.

Daily List Writing

Each morning, before you dive into your day, engage the power of the Universe by writing down what you want to do, what you want to happen, and what you want to receive. Yup, including Magic Money.

You can do this in your Magic Money Journal, on a notepad, or even on a napkin. The important thing is that you do it before you get too far into your day.

You see, without intention, your subconscious mind produces a conglomeration of miscellaneous desires. Maybe something great will happen, maybe not. By setting clear intentions, your subconscious mind combines with the unseen powers of the Universe to produce your desires. Sounds great, right? *It is*. And it's as easy as it appears to be.

Remember Experimenter Julia in *Beginning Magic Money*? She's in retail sales and has a side hustle (a network marketing business). She's a former single mom (note the "former," thanks to adding *find the love of my life* to her Master List), and now a homeowner! Well, she's also super cool and offered to share one of her daily lists (results in parenthesis):

Saturday, November 14, 2015

I am so happy and grateful now that:

- *I feel healthy and strong today.* (She had been a bit under the weather and wanted to manifest great health that day.)

- *I received a large sum of unexpected money to pay for my son's braces.* (Later that day, she checked her bank balance and noticed she received a $2,557 bonus from being a top achiever at her day job.)

- *I attract one recruit into my business.* (She signed up a guy named Jake, who not only turned out to be incredible, he's building an entire leg in her downline, and she's making a few extra thousands of dollars per month already, just seven months later.)

- *I sell more than $3,500 in product today at work.* (She sold $3,136 in product that day. It is important to note the average daily sales performance in her store is $500, and that day it was $471, making her about a zillion percent more awesome than her peers.)

By sitting down at a set time every day, and writing what your intentions and ideas of good are for that day, you will find that much if not all of what you want will come to you. The act of writing down what you want creates clarity, helps you define what you truly want, and will get good results for you.

Dr. Emmet Fox said, *This is the way to alter your life, writing out what you want to experience in your life.*

Think about it for a second, just the act of writing down what you want, either on your Master List or Daily List, sets the wheels in motion and can help more of what you want to come to you quickly, easily, and effortlessly. I mean, how cool is that? I have been doing this practice now for more than 20 years, and I'm still blown away by the combination of its simplicity and effectiveness.

I would be remiss if I didn't mention something else at play here: if you *don't* get definite about what you want in writing, you are in essence drifting along and could manifest anything, or nothing.

And there is another possibility, too, and you won't love it. Without setting a clear, written intention, it is possible you will manifest what stronger personalities around you desire. This is because you become a broadcasting station for what they want. Sometimes we bring into our lives what those around us want when we aren't clear and purposeful about what we want. A simple example is when you end up at a restaurant eating what someone else wanted for dinner because you didn't say *tacos*. (Never give up the opportunity to weigh in and have a taco. Never.)

List-Making in Action

You've already thought of something you want, and hopefully, you wrote it down. To fully set your intention as part of your Second Magic Money Experiment, get definite about it by writing it out in specific detail. Take as long as you need, be specific, and be confident! The act of writing it down will allow you to crystallize your true desire.

When you're writing down your intention, write it as thought you were filling out the "what I already have" section of an insurance document. If your insurance company was going to replace your desire, how would they know what to replace?

Just as I mentioned you could become a broadcasting station for what someone else wants, by writing down your desires you become a broadcasting station for what you want. Writing your desires intentionally broadcasts exactly what you want, thereby multiplying the likelihood you get it!

The specific reason you should get definite about what you want is this: the word desire means "of the Father." Any deep-seeded desire you desire is a universal desire for good. It is the Universe's great pleasure to give it to you, and it should be your great pleasure to receive it.

As I mentioned, if your desires are surface desires (as opposed to something you want and will still want later), they will eventually pass. The deep-seeded desires will remain with you until they manifest. You should express them constructively in writing, and memorialize what you want. When you don't, you are suppressing your desires. That means they may not come to you no matter how much you want them (a.k.a. *not good!*)

When you think *That would never happen for me,* you are suppressing your deep-seeded desires. When you write about what you want, tangibles and intangibles, they are most likely to occur. The universe wants to give you what you want, just as much as you want to receive it.

To this day, in my Magic Money Journal, I take a few minutes every morning to jot down what I'd like to happen that day. I suggest you utilize the magical power of list making to not only bring more magic money into your life but to bring other magical items, events, and other wonderful surprises as well!

When you begin to write about what you want, you become definite about what you want. I believe this works for a few reasons.

One, clarity is power. When you remove all doubt as to what you want, you open the way for it to come to you. Uncertain intentions bring unpredictable results. Ultimately, what you want can come to you, when you are clear about what it is you *do* want.

Two, there is incredible power in the written word. The brain-body connection activates, and the spiritual aspect comes into play. Finally, writing down what you want allows you to get it out of your mind and onto paper. Again, you write it as if it is already done, in a grateful way, which removes any feelings of lack or longing.

It is true that a state of lack and longing prevents the good you desire from manifesting. Become clear about what you want, and memorialize it in writing to clear out any confusion or uncertainty. Your desire will come to pass faster and easier.

Every day (at least once a day) I add to and check off items on my Master and Daily Lists. The more you play around with the concepts, the better you'll become at your list making to create what you want in your life.

Choice Produces Results

Remember this: choice produces results. If you do not choose something positive and constructive, through omission, you are choosing lack and limitation and confusion. You must use choice at all times, either deliberate choice for something good or no choice which is actually choosing whatever comes to you. And I can guarantee you when you practice daily list-making, you will shortly be overwhelmed by the amount of goodness that flows into your life.

Here's why: your definite written words eliminate or dissolve all obstacles and barriers on the visible and invisible plains of life. Your definite written words open the way for your desired good to come to you through people, circumstances, and events. Your definite, written words open the way for what you want to come to you. Hopefully, you are convinced and have already taken at least one small break to write a few desires on your Master List. If you haven't, now is a great time!

Amber is a childhood friend of mine. We reconnected a little under four years ago through, where else, Facebook! Today, she's an artist who designs logos and branding campaigns for small businesses. When I shared this concept with her, she was skeptical (and rightly so, it does sound simple and easy, I'll give you that). She proved this concept for herself with her design services. Before talking to me, she received several different (and somewhat opposing) opinions about why she wasn't engaging more business. Then, she started using the list-making technique, but initially didn't put it on her list anything about engaging new clients. When I asked her about it, on her next day's list, she put *I am so happy and grateful now that I have engaged two new clients at my full fee at the perfect times, in the right ways.* That afternoon, she was given a referral, and the following Friday, another client came through her website.

Psychologists tell us that most things are done through choice. Everywhere we turn, we're encouraged to *Awaken the Giant Within* (Anthony Robbins) or *Choose Yourself* (James Altucher). It's true, choice produces results, and it is up to you to make the choice about what you want—*in writing.*

Because they are such excellent ways to set intentions, you can become amazingly wealthy or receive any of your other desires in an easy, quiet way through the Master List and Daily List Writing techniques.

Here are a few more things to keep in mind:

Take your list-making seriously.

Just like ordering from Amazon, you're serious when you press the Buy Now button and expect to receive your goods. The list-making techniques are no different: when you write something down, expect to receive it. You're asking for what you want, and as I've said, it is the Universe's great pleasure to bring it to you. When you ask, ask with your whole mind, heart, and soul and expect to receive it!

Be as specific as possible.

Be fearless when writing down exactly what you want. Over the years, I've graduated to asking for what I truly want, and only what I truly want.

Allow me to share some backstory. Before I wrapped my brain around the concept of asking for what I wanted, no matter how big, crazy, or seemingly unobtainable, I would try to work out in my mind how what I wanted might find its way to me. How I might be able to afford the nicer car, bigger home, a more expensive computer. If I couldn't see a clear path to buying or receiving

41

what I wanted with my current conditions, I would often look for a "more realistic" or less expensive option. For what seemed like the longest time, I didn't allow myself to dream as big as I wanted to, and was instead willing to settle for what I thought I could get.

Please don't do that! Save yourself some time and other not-so-great emotional experiences by just skipping right to asking for what you want and then getting on with your day, positively expecting it to show up.

Remember: Just as we have disproven: "money must come to me through my job," you can receive your desires through just about any channel.

Stay unattached.

Like almost all intentions, stay unattached to the timing or even the outcome. As the saying goes, *Timing is everything,* and it is true when practicing the Magic Money Philosophy. As you open your mind to manifesting, earning, receiving, and caring for your magic money (and other goodies), it is important to detach from not just the how but also the when. You will increase your ability to get all of them faster! Eventually you will be able to receive them instantly, as I discuss in *Magic Money Mastery*.

I know once you want something, or even when you need more money, you want it now. And you want it exactly the way you picture it in your mind, or in the exact amount you need (or an additional $5, so you can get an ice cream). I understand. As you now know, there is an absolute abundance that surrounds you and is available to and for you. *Sometimes*, dare I say *most of the time*, the amount of money that comes flowing to you far exceeds what you had in mind. The "thing" you asked for can pale in comparison to what shows up.

With the implementation of the Magic Money Philosophy, you are now "smart-at-work" (as opposed to hard at work) on expanding your magic money consciousness to make it as unlimited as possible.

You hear about people who "have more money than they could spend in ten lifetimes." Now that's an expanded magic money consciousness, and that is exactly what I have in mind for you! You might be asking for enough money to pay cash for a new set of wheels, when in fact at any moment the Universe might, and could, deliver enough for you to buy an entire car dealership. To the Universe, they are the same thing. The only contributing difference would be your magic money setting.

In other words, if the most you *think* you can attract, manifest, or allow into your life is just enough to pay for the thing or event you want, that's most likely what you're going to receive. The Universe won't expand past your current consciousness. If you continue to expand what you think is possible for you, the Universe will expand with you and rise to meet you.

Sounds amazing, right? It is!

When I first moved to New York City more than twenty years ago, I lived a block away from an Ann Taylor clothing store. I just could not imagine who might be rich enough to pay a whole $99 for a suit jacket. I mean, whoa! Now, without blinking an eye, I will spend whatever I need to when I'm purchasing a suit jacket (and it is a whole lot more than $99 these days)! I grew up where the big clothing store in town was a Fashion Bug in a strip mall, so I had some consciousness expanding to do.

I'm not saying there's anything wrong with thinking Fashion Bug is cool, or even expensive, or that Ann Taylor isn't just too far out of the budget. Because there isn't: whatever you think is big enough or perfect for you *is*. What I am saying is that if you can think it, dream about it, and dare to ask for it, you can have it. There are, as I've shared, some internal actions you now know you take. Of course, there are also some *external* actions you'll need to take, but we're not there quite yet.

First, let's talk about another powerful and effective way to set your intention: *visualization*.

Chapter Four

SETTING YOUR INTENTION *WITH VISUALIZATION*

Another way to set, and realize, your intentions is through the practice of visualization. Visualization is, very simply, a mental movie. But this movie is extra cool because it is the movie you are playing in your mind.

And just like writing down what you want, there are different ways to utilize visualization to its fullest. Let's start with the one you can probably try right now.

47

The Fast and Fabulous: 60 Seconds

Using your mind and energy to bring about what you want doesn't take very long. Thank goodness, because there are some days I am busy from morning until night, without much of a break. That's when I use the "fast and fabulous" visualization option.

Here's something awesome you might not know: Hold your intention in your mind for just sixty seconds (yes, just one minute) without wavering or allowing any negative thoughts, and you will be able to manifest anything you want. And it will usually appear almost instantaneously!

Sounds easy right? I thought so, too, until I tried it. In the beginning, it can be pretty challenging to hold a pure, positive thought for even ten seconds, much less for a whole minute! You know exactly what you want because you can already picture it in your mind. You're just a few Fast and Fabulous Sixty Second Visualizations away from the Universe understanding exactly what you want and aligning people, things, and events to bring it to you.

So how do you get the Fast and Fabulous Sixty Second Visualization to work for you? The same way you get to Carnegie Hall: practice, practice, practice!

You know by now I'm not going to leave you hanging, and I'm going to explain precisely what I mean when I say "practice."

When I say practice, I first mean identifying an amount of money you desire or something on your list. Next, create a clear picture of a check, a stack or pile of money, or the item you want and make sure it is "in action" (i.e., not a static picture). Imagine getting a mobile notification that amount of money is in your account, or the item you want has been delivered. In your mental movie, imagine how you will feel the moment you realize what you want is now yours: Perhaps excited! Relieved! Thrilled! Overwhelmed with joy!

I don't know how you'd feel; I only know how I feel: blissed out beyond belief. In my Fast and Fabulous Sixty Second Visualizations: I imagine the money I want or the thing I desire as being in my possession and let my imagination run wild from there. For exactly sixty seconds.

I'm asking you to visualize what you want as already yours, and perhaps even imagining how it makes its way to you. It is important for me

49

to point out that most of the time you will have no idea or influence regarding the channel. The money will show up in a surprising way, or the item you've set your heart on will make its way to you through a surprising channel.

One Minute to Magic Money

How do I know a minute has elapsed? I use the built-in countdown timer in my phone. I set the timer and do the visualization over and over until the timer goes off. Done and done. When the timer goes off, I'm pretty hopped up on the endorphins in my system. Then, I get on with whatever I was doing before the visualization, fully expecting what I've visualized will show up in the perfect time in the perfect way.

Utilizing visualization to your highest potential is the same as using the GPS (Global Positioning System) you have in your car. Plug in your destination and the GPS identifies that fastest way to get you where you want to go, and you're off.

Holding your desire in mind for sixty seconds is like programming the Universal GPS, and you can do this practice any time you have sixty seconds.

Let's identify just a few of the sixty-second periods you have throughout the day:

- While you're waiting for your morning coffee or tea to brew.

- While you're drying off after your morning shower.

- During any television commercial break.

- While you're at a stoplight.

- As you're brushing your teeth.

A visualization practice doesn't require any special gear, clothing, locations, or skills. You can visualize several times a day, anywhere you happen to be, on a moment's notice. I highly encourage you to practice your one-minute visualizations as often as humanly possible. These intentional daydreams are a terrific use of your time, and not only do they work, but they are also fun, and you will enjoy doing them!

One important reason to engage in a sixty-second visualization practice multiple times per day is to counter-act other things you might be doing to slow down or stop the Magic Money and other awesomeness that might otherwise show up for you. The truth is the average person rarely finishes a single sentence without stopping a manifestation before it could ever come to pass. For example, in one sentence most people state what they want (set an intention), and then immediately stop it in its tracks. For example: *I really want a brand new BMW 325i, but it is much too expensive for me.*

I don't know about you, but I wasn't taught to say simply, *I really want a brand new BMW 325i*, and then let the Universe figure out how to bring it to me.

I was taught I needed to know how I was going to pay for it first. I've since learned all of that mental pre-planning and stress is frankly unnecessary. It is astounding and life changing to realize you have the power within you to create anything and everything you want. It's up to you to make this realization and decide the easy way over the hard way. But more on that in *Magic Money Mastery.*

Quiet Time Ritual

In his book, *The Power of Consistency,* Weldon Long shares his visualization process, the Quiet Time Ritual. Originally a book for sales and business professionals, I stumbled upon this read through Amazon's "also bought" section. I downloaded the audiobook and was entranced as Weldon shared his tough story, one which has left him today in a place of triumph and abundance.

Using his *Quiet Time Ritual* strategy, I crafted a fifteen-minute daily ritual for creating and manifesting the life I desired. To that end, I wrote out a detailed description of my life as I would like it to be and review it during (you guessed it), my nightly Quiet Time Ritual (QTR). Just like the intentions you set in writing, crafting an overall life vision in writing is to your highest and best advantage.

I've found reading through my positive statements and descriptions on a twice-daily basis keeps my desires at the forefront of my mind. The added cool bonus is my list keeps changing, because as I add desires, I see others that have manifested. I give thanks and then remove or replace them.

Daily visualization in the form of the Quiet Time Ritual is an enjoyable, fun, and easy process *that works wonders*. You'll want to read Mr. Long's book and craft your own ideal life, in writing, too.

Easier than You Think

If you're stuck on how you might train your mind to positively focus for sixty whole seconds an intended desire, fifteen minutes might be too much to grasp at this moment. But stay with me here, because there is such power in performing a ritual that contains within it the ability to take you from wherever you are right now and compel you into a life you've designed.

Let me warn and excite you at the same time: the QTR not only works in wondrous ways, it works fast! Like I mentioned, I have been practicing my QTR for the better part of three years. I have had to change and update my description on a half-dozen occasions—every single time it was because as I was reading what I wanted to bring into my life, I realized *I already had it.*

Sometimes it had just come to pass, other times I realized it had just happened, and I needed to update my QTR in real time.

While I'll leave you to read the book to create your QTR, let me give you a few shortcuts and a couple of finer points I've learned:

- By consistently picturing what you desire, combining focus with emotion, you will ultimately be empowered to, and desire to take the necessary action to bring about what you want (all aided by the power of the Universe).

- Doing the QTR right before you fall asleep gives your subconscious mind the time it needs to give your desires the attention they need. It's also great to think of inspiring and positive things as you fall asleep (when your subconscious mind is most receptive).

- To never miss a session, I have my QTR in Evernote on all my devices: iPhone, iPad, and computer. The very last thing I do each night before going to sleep is review my QTR written statement.

Now I'm not going to say I've left the best intention-setting and manifesting approach for last, yet I do believe our words, the ones we speak out loud, are magical and should be treated as such. Just when you think the Magic Money Philosophy can't get any better, I promise you, you're in for a treat!

Chapter Five

SETTING YOUR INTENTION *THROUGH YOUR WORDS*

Many years ago, I read a book by Shad Helmstetter, *What to Say When You Talk to Yourself*. Once I completed that book, I attempted to be mindful of my words. For the first time, I had insight and a basic understanding of the power of my words. Then I stumbled upon *Your Word is Your Wand* by Florence Scovel Shinn, *The Dynamic Laws of Prosperity* by Catherine Ponder, and more recently, two books by Pam Grout: *E-Squared* and *E-Cubed*.

These books had a similar message: *what you say is what you get.*

These books opened the true possibilities to me, and reminded me over and over that what you say when you talk to yourself is heard not only by your subconscious mind, or even by others, the Universe hears your words, too.

Which is why I saved *speaking* to set your intentions for last. We could spend many hours discussing which among these three tactics of writing, visualizing, or speaking is the most important or even the most useful. While I think all of them are equally as important, I would bet all the money in the world that the next thing you do is say something, as opposed to writing or visualizing. Which means you are creating your financial situation, your relationships, work, and every little thing about your life every time you utter a sound.

Take a moment and let it sink in. *Every word you utter shapes your outer world, so you best think something positive before you speak, positively.*

When you say things like, *I can't afford that,* or *That could never happen for me*, even if no-one else is listening, you can bet your subconscious mind and the Universe are hanging on every word. As I've mentioned, it is the Universe's great pleasure to give you your heart's desire, and it makes no distinction between one positive statement from the next.

But, you're thinking, saying *I can't afford that* isn't a positive statement. Isn't it? Isn't anything you say a statement of what you want, a verbal command to the Universe?

Oh, wait. *It is* (which can be a frightening and sobering realization). But wait! Recognizing how powerful your words can be—are—is incredibly awesome, too!

In fact, everything you say is a positive statement, a directive, to be carried out as quickly as possible. Every statement you make is an affirmation, yet perhaps what you are affirming isn't exactly what you have in mind.

An affirmation is anything you say, and repeat when you speak. Affirmations are considered *positive statements that bring about what we want.* When you say, over and over, *I am always late*, or *That always happens to me*, you are making an affirmation. But I'm sure if I could ask you right now, you would say you don't want always to be late, and you don't want whatever that not-so-good thing is that always happen to you to continue happening to you. Right? Right.

I'm sure at this point the clouds are parting, and you are having the realization that as you have been saying that thing you've been saying *for years* (repeatedly), you've been creating that thing (whatever it is). And, you just want to kick yourself.

Well, don't do that. Instead, just keep reading. Now that you know better, you'll do better.

Your casual words, you may have previously believed, were simply that: casual (and therefore had no unintended consequences). That the affirmative statements you've intended to say could, and should, be stronger than anything "negative" you might have said in any random moment. Except that your words, whether casual or intentional, seek their reality.

The time has come for you to stop and think before you speak.

From this day forward, I challenge you to say exactly, and only, what you want to become your reality.

I'm going to shoot straight with you: this could be the single biggest challenge of your life so far.

I want to make sure you hear me now: if you can master your words, you can master your destiny.

Crafting powerful, intentional thoughts and statements with your written words and creative visualization, and you will be a manifesting ninja the likes of which have never been seen before!

I'm sure you'd like some things you can put into practice immediately because I know you want to become an even more awesome manifesting ninja immediately if not sooner. I mean, who doesn't want that?!

The formula I'm about to give you comes in handy in just about every challenging situation you encounter, in addition to being a powerful way to set intentions and receive desired results. And, I'm giving it to you in three simple steps:

Step One.

Say what you want and only what you want. If, by some chance, you hear yourself

61

uttering something you don't want to become your reality, say *Cancel, cancel, cancel!!* Then, take a moment and say what you do want.

Example: You send a proposal out to a prospective client, and you say, *It will be a miracle if that happens. I can think of sixty-four reasons why I won't get selected for the contract.* Then you realize, *Oh, crap, that isn't what I want at all! I want them to immediately engage me, at my full fee, by the end of the month.* Take a moment, collect your thoughts, and then say something like this, *I am so happy and grateful now that XYZ Company engages me at my full fee immediately. We have a wonderful time working together, for the good of all concerned.* Then add this: *This or something even better!* Stay with me; I'll get to *This or something better* in a second.

Step Two.

If, at any time, something appears *not* to be working out the way you intend, <u>remain unmoved</u> and hand the relationship or situation over to the Universe. You can do that with your words, in writing, or even with a 60-second visualization. If you're feeling inspired, do all three.

You might be wondering what *remain unmoved* means, so I'll tell you exactly: no matter how dire the situation, no matter how challenging, or bleak, or disastrous it seems to be, don't get upset, spun up, angry, frustrated, or sad. *Remain unmoved* means you keep it steady, remain calm, and focus on your desired outcome. Do your very best to feel how you will feel when the situation works out in a magical way. Because engaging in this three-step process means that it will!

Now at some point, you may be inspired to take an action of some sort, or, alternatively, just "hang ten" until you get your desired result. As you remain calm, it might occur to you that there is some action you can take to get the result you want. That is known as inspired action, and if it feels right to you, go on ahead and do it. If you're the slightest bit unsure, just wait for your next intuitive hit, or get busy doing something else while the Universe works it out for you.

Example: I was attempting to put a book up for pre-order recently. For some reason, my account on Amazon was blocked for pre-orders (something about missing a deadline, and I can tell you, *I do not miss deadlines!* I mean, if you knew me, you would absolutely swear on a stack of chocolate chip pancakes this is, indeed, the case.) Anyway, not putting this book up for presale was Not. An. Option. In fact, the book needed to be up for pre-order and within the next three days. So, I reached out to customer service, and got the answer I wanted: *Holly, you are go for launch, baby!* Yay, I thought! Problem solved!

But nope, my joy was short-lived because when I tried again, no pre-sale for me. So, I handed the situation over to the Universe and got on with my day. About an hour later, it occurred to me there was one contact I had that could help. With my fingers and toes crossed, and another short conversation with the Universe (*Hey Universe, it would be really great if you could work this out and quickly! Thanks so much! K, bye bye!*) took the action I was inspired to take (in this case, send an email to someone who might be able to help), and resolved the situation within 24 hours. A successful pre-sale and launch proceeded without any other hitches in my giddy-up. Whew!

Step Three.

In addition to remaining unmoved, it's also a stellar idea to remain unattached to the outcome. About 95% of the time, the Universe shows off by delivering what you've asked for with some extra goodies like whipped cream and a cherry on top. The Universe crushes it, making magic and miracles happen as easily as buying a candy bar out of a vending machine. But every so often I want something and the answer I get is a simple *Nope, sorry Holly, no deal.* I used to lose faith in "the system." I would get all riled up because I was a card-carrying member of the Magic Money Philosophy and then it would seem that the "Law of Attraction" was out to lunch or on vacation. I mean, by its very name, should work every time, no exceptions because it's a freaking *law*.

But I have learned, instead of getting upset in any way, to instead get excited—because the Universe tends to have something up its proverbial sleeve I like *even better* and I can't wait to see what it's going to be! I have learned to maintain my zen-like state, the sweet combination of remaining unmoved and unattached, and to sit back and enjoy a hot fudge sundae while I let the powers that be *do their thang*. Because try as I might, and even with my super powers of imagination, I can't dream as big as the Universe. Nor can I see just how the Universe is going to magically and synchronistically orchestrate everything to work out perfectly in my favor.

It always does, right on time, in the most amazing ways. Trust me; you're going to love how the Universe always has your back and comes through again and again.

If, on the off chance, you find yourself falling into doubt or fear, do the steps from your First Magic Money Experiment in a big way. And while you're at it, write down what you want. Speak some words of affirmation. Do a few Fast and Fabulous Sixty Second Visualizations.

The Power of the Right Questions

I hinted to something else that's awesome about the Magic Money Philosophy above, and it is this: when something "bad" happens, I know better than to determine right in that moment it is, indeed, bad.

You can, from this point forward, take any personal or professional crisis and recognize it contains within it the seeds of opportunity.

The end of a marriage (friendship, relationship, or partnership), losing a job, even a personal health crisis seems (and can be) awful. Especially in those first few moments and days when trying to wrap your brain around a situation you might have thought was "a given." *Of course we are going to be married forever,* or *I thought I was performing above company standards,* or *I take excellent care of myself, how did this happen!?* can quickly cause strong emotions and, frankly, a sense of panic.

Without question, you will move through the emotional stages of denial, anger, bargaining, and depression, perhaps several times before you are able to truly land in acceptance. I'm not at all diminishing that these emotional stages are real, or that your physical situation isn't a big deal. However, I do think we have more power over our thoughts and emotions. To that end, part of the Magic Money Philosophy is to deal with anything that comes our way head on, to rise to the occasion as opposed to just riding the wave of emotions as they come.

It takes practice to, say exactly and only what you want, while remaining unmoved and unattached, especially in the face of something you absolutely do *not* want. It takes almost a moment-by-moment reminder we are not victims, at the mercy of others or some unseen force, and instead able to direct what happens next with our thoughts, words, mental pictures, and emotions.

You might have a situation in mind as you question my unwavering positive focus, perhaps thinking, *But you've never had THIS situation, Holly, you just can't know my pain and suffering.* You're right, I don't know what challenges you might have encountered in your life, but I can share just a few of mine:

- I was beaten, nearly to death, on three separate occasions by my father. I spent a week in critical care on one occasion, which resulted in ...

- being placed in foster care. After being notified by my school I had "ditched (not attended) a day of classes" my male caretaker had me dig my grave (2.5 feet wide, by 8 feet long, by 6 feet deep (which took all night) as punishment. I hadn't ditched at all, it was a clerical mistake.

- After graduating high school, I worked at least three jobs at one time for a few years (until: Magic Money!) to make ends meet.

• Not surprisingly, I married a verbally abusive husband. When our daughter was very young, he left me for another woman. I became a single mom with no familial support.

Those are just four of the (give-or-take) one hundred or so things I could list. When I say, *I understand*, I do. I might not understand exactly what you are going through, or have gone through, but *I get it*. And when I say it takes practice to remain positive, unmoved and focused—and that it really works—it is because I have had lots and lots and lots (I mean, seriously, *lots*) of practice.

In addition to the above three steps, I've developed a few questions I call Positive Power Questions (PPQs). I ask them when I realize I'm in a situation and it feels beyond my control.

I start with: *What else could this mean?* It might take you a few hours, days or weeks to have a moment of sanity and ask this question, and that's okay. Nothing truly means anything except the meaning we give it. If you can take a challenge and give it an alternate, more positive (or even neutral) meaning, you're going to feel more in control and at peace.

Recently, one of my advisors had a long-time partnership end. After being in business with one partner for five years, they opted to take on two other partners who, as the saying goes, "Looked good on paper." These two additional partners seemed to have the ability to grow the overall business exponentially, and there was an overall spirit of optimism about the future.

It didn't take long for the two original partners to see the writing on the wall. While their business efforts yielded huge gains, the two newer partners were not only *not* bringing in new revenues to the company, they had commanded huge signing bonuses and salaries. All the increased business went to pay for the additional overhead instead of putting more money in my friends' pockets.

When I asked *What else could this mean?* There were several fantastic answers: *they were more than enough on their own. They didn't need additional people who had more years and experience to grow the partnership.* This led to a resolution to end the partnership, and today the business has the two original partners knocking it out of the park, making more money, and doing better than ever.

We've already covered in depth the question: *What do I want to happen?* and you now know after you decide what you want, it is then time to set your intention.

I've included a few other questions I tend to use, depending on the situation I'm faced with:

Is it possible this is for the best?

If you've ever been in a marriage, friendship, partnership, or job where you haven't been miserable but you haven't been happy, you have probably been simultaneously relieved and fearful when it ended abruptly. Ask yourself if it's possible, even probable the end is for the best can help you reframe what the event means to you.

I follow the above question with this: *Have I been ignoring any signs?*

You just might, with a short period of reflection, connect some dots you hadn't connected before—see things you hadn't previously seen. If the answer is yes, it opens the way for further analysis of how this bad thing is a blessing in disguise.

Another terrific PPQ: *What don't I know yet?*

First, you don't know how everything is going to work out! You can't know quite yet just how the Universe is conspiring on your behalf, lining up people, circumstances, events, *and money* to bring you to the right place, at the right time, with the right people. All you can do it ask the question, *What don't I know yet?* and allow what else you need to know to be revealed to you.

Asking yourself PPQs forces you to give yourself positive, powerful answers—ask yourself a terrible question (*Why does this always happen to me?*), and you'll feel terrible. That's why I suggest writing down these questions, which are purposely worded to put, and keep, you in a resourceful place, and keep them handy. Write them in the front of your journal, or make them into an Evernote document you can access from anywhere. Have a friend remind you to consult your PPQs when you find yourself faced with any situation, big or small.

There's one final PPQ you just might find the most useful and helpful of all. I believe the very best thing you can do in a crisis is determine who you have as a resource.

Ask yourself, *Who can help me?*

You probably have a parent, friend, colleague, or professional connection with the skills to help.

I'm an incredibly private person and keep most of my problems to myself, sometimes *only* to myself. You have a tiny glimpse into my background, and those challenges have shaped who I am. But how I deal with things is not always the healthiest, and it has taken quite a bit of work for me not only to practice the techniques I'm sharing with you, but to also allow them to help.

Do not keep your biggest challenges to yourself! I don't advise you to tell everyone, or to post them on Facebook, or even constantly discuss them. My best tip for you: identify who you have in your corner. Tell them what's going on, what you're up against—*once*. Then, allow them to provide counsel, advice, encouragement, and words of assurance. Ask them to ask you your PPQs, to help keep you focused on the positive, and remind you of all of the other good in your life.

Your fastest way through any challenge or obstacle is to identify exactly what's not right, determine how you want it to be, and then seek the advice of someone who can help you make the most progress in the least amount of time. Take in what they say, process it and listen to your gut about what you can, should, or must do to come through it in the best way possible.

Now that you have the PPQs in your toolbox, you'll find practicing the finer points of the Magic Money Philosophy more effortless. There's another facet I haven't yet shared with you, and the time has come to share it with you. I know you're gonna love it!

Bless Everything as Good

A powerful piece of the Magic Money Philosophy is to *bless everything as good*. This is particularly easy when something good happens! It's even easy to bless something as simple as a meal, which is neither positive nor negative, although something you have probably practiced on a regular basis for some or most of your life.

What about when you are facing something that seems insurmountable? When something appears to be going wrong, do you curse it or

74

bless it? Our natural reaction is often to talk about it endlessly, complain and curse it, but that only serves to create more anxiety and stress (in addition to more things to get upset about!).

There is a common step you can take, perhaps one you've done thousands of times, without realizing it's true power: *declare a blessing*. If you say a blessing before you eat, you've been using this technique. Saying a prayer or a blessing over our meals is common practice. But perhaps you didn't realize you can declare a blessing for every single thing and aspect of your life. You can bless what you already have. You can bless what you want to bring into your life. And, you can bless what you don't want as good, and this act can alter the situation for the better.

I learned about blessing people and situations many years ago though Catherine Ponder in her book, *The Dynamic Secrets of the Ages*. A blessing is a very simple way to say a positive prayer for someone or something. One of Catherine Ponder's favorite blessings is *I bless you and bless you for the goodness of God that is within you.*

Through blessing, we offer our positive thoughts of good with the intention they will return to us multiplied. When you send positive thoughts and vibrations toward a person, thing, or event, they are likely to respond in kind. You are always best served to offer a blessing than to send a curse!

How to Bless Anything and Everything as Good

Just as when you offer a meal blessing, you can do the same in any situation. *I bless this situation/person as good! May it be resolved for the good of all concerned, in an easy way, with perfect timing.*

Offering a blessing can be used in a wonderful way in all sorts of situations:

Number One.

When you are angry or frustrated at someone. Bless the person and see them as peaceful and happy, and the situation between you resolved.

Number Two.

If you are experiencing pain or illness, bless your health as good and resolved. You can bless yourself and your own emotions, too.

Number Three.

A difficult boss, co-worker, employee, or partner may leave or transfer after you have blessed them and the situation. They might even shift the way they are behaving toward you because the act of offering is a blessing truly is magical and can cause a seemingly inexplicable change in emotions and behaviors right before your very eyes.

Number Four.

Bless your taxes, bills, debts, and creditors and thank them for the service they provide. An important part of the Magic Money Philosophy, giving these blessings contributes to always having the money to pay them on time.

Number Five.

Be sure to bless your travels and see them going smoothly and magically. In all my years of driving and flying, I've only been delayed a handful of times—and never when I had to be somewhere.

Number Six.

Bless politicians, especially if you want to do the opposite and curse them. Politicians and all other people in a position of leadership need to be blessed with the wisdom to make the best decisions for all that they serve. As with blessing anything, blessing them will do so much more than complaining about them.

Number Seven.

When you're out in the world, bless people as you pass them. Bless others on the roads you drive, in the stores you shop, and in the restaurants you eat. I silently bless everyone and everything while I'm waiting. It makes the time pass by, and I rarely encounter awkward or challenging situations while I'm out.

Number Eight.

I've left the best for last: bless your most significant relationships, those with your family and closest friends. Say a blessing for them as often as you think of them, for all the good and especially for any hurts. Relationships can improve when they are good, or heal quickly when you begin blessing them.

You can bless any situation as good, and as the act of blessing shifts how you feel about it, the changes it creates can seem magical.

Emmet Fox said: *Bless a thing, and it will bless you. Curse a thing, and it will curse you. If you put your condemnation upon anything in life, it will hit back at you and hurt you. If you bless a situation, it has no power to hurt you and even if it is troublesome, for a time, it will gradually fade out, if you sincerely bless it.*

Remember this: happy people aren't mean, spiteful, vengeful, or rude. You can't change them, but you can send them blessings. If they become happy, they will change their behavior, and everyone wins! Even if things don't suddenly shift with the person or situation being blessed, you will feel better once you have been able to bless them. Never underestimate the power of blessing someone or something as good.

Remind yourself often: *The act of blessing has multiplying power. As I bless what is on hand, this opens the way for it to increase mightily. I bless and increase my health, wealth, and happiness now!*

Everything is a Sign of Awesomeness

You might be wondering, with all this magic and miracles talk, how I explain any bad things that happen. I've decided to adopt a few beliefs in my life, and one of them is this:

When something good happens, I take that as a sign more good things are in the works. More blessings are on their way. When something not-to-good happens, I take that as a sign that something good (better! Much better!) is about to happen.

Know this: not everything bad that happens is actually a bad thing.

Case in point: a girlfriend of mine, Katy, decided to test out some of this "magic money stuff" I was sharing with her. She knew she was undercharging for her services, did some checking around and learned others with less experience and time on the job were making double or even triple what she was. She is a freelancer, and at the end of her contract, let her biggest client know she was doubling her rates. When they talked, he said *I'll think about it.* When she hung up the phone, she was absolutely sure he was going to call back, *You're worth every dime! I accept your raise—and you're pretty!* Instead, he fired her.

Meanwhile, it turns out the Universe had been patiently waiting for her to own her greatness and raise her rates. Because some other folks had been introduced to her work and fell in love with her style, spirit, and skills. But they knew if they tried to hire her, it would be considered poaching by their friend, her client. They wrote on *their* lists, We want Katy as our full-time person. Not someone like her, *her*. If only she were available, we would hire her in a minute and pay her whatever she wants, because she's *that good.*

So she ends up in the city where they lived and was lamenting over lunch how she'd gotten all inspired to raise her rates and then had gotten fired. *And they hired her on the spot. Right then. At her full fee.*

When she told me she needed to talk over coffee *right away,* I was immediately concerned. She was newly pregnant with her second child, and her husband's business has been on a roller-coaster of sorts. I had no idea what in the world we were talking about: were we going to celebrate something, or would I be playing the role of good supportive girlfriend, bringing chocolate and a cozy sweater?

Well, it turns out I needn't have worried. The Universe had my back, too, and worked its magic to give her just a glimpse of its, and her, capabilities.

This or Something Better

When you set an intention for something, keep in mind something I mentioned earlier: the Universe has no limits and can bring much bigger and better results than anything we can conceive. You think, *I'd love a raise so I can afford the payments on a new car*, while the Universe is thinking, *Let's give him a new car, paid in full.* You wonder, *Is it possible we could afford to spend two weeks in Europe?* While the Universe is planning *a year in Europe, all expenses paid.*

When I ask for something, I also have a little side convo with the Universe, *I'm totally clear you're in charge and might have something better in mind. Have at it; I'm going to get back to minding my own business.* Like I've mentioned, every day I write down all of the cool things that come my way.

You're not limited to what you can think up, and what you manifest can be multiples better than your imagination can sometimes cook up.

Whew! We've covered a lot of ground in this chapter. I've pulled out all the stops because I want you to feel like you know the way to Easy Street. In fact, know this: you're already on it! And, if you ever get lost, you can find your way back almost as quickly as Dorothy clicked her heels in the Wizard of Oz.

Now that you know how to set your intentions in multiple ways let's get on with creating more actual Magic Money in your life (and wallet).

Chapter Six

MORE MAGIC MONEY MAXIMIZATION

I f it has been more than thirty days since you have had the chance to read *Beginning Magic Money,* specifically Chapter Four: Magic Money Maximization, I encourage you to go back and give it a quick read. The purpose of that chapter was to sow some magic money seeds into your life. I was intentionally preparing you, more specifically your subconscious mind, there was another way, a magical way, to handle money.

85

Up until this point, I have only suggested there is way to handle your money so you can maximize it. I've kept you focused on what I know to be the basis for massive wealth and abundance: a magic money mindset.

Once your mindset is on point, you must then handle your money with intention and purpose. You must manage your money in a way that provides you with the most amount of joy and the least amount of stress. What do I mean? Here's a hint: give, save, have fun with, pay off debt, and prepare for expenses like taxes.

Combine your thoughts and words with magic money actions, and you are going to step squarely into the magic of having, *and I mean always having from this point forward*, an abundance of money.

You now know how to maximize your mindset and put yourself in the flow of money. You have had a glimpse into how to handle your money as it comes in. Let's go a step further and get you ready for your Second Magic Money Experiment.

To get, and stay in the flow of magic money, you must make up your mind to trust the process. It is in your moments of decision you shape your destiny. To fully become the abundant being I know you can be, you must make the decision to see things as you desire them to be, even in the face of what might seem the exact opposite of what you want. When you speak about and visualize things as you want them to be, or feel fear, doubt, or frustration and continue to engage in the Magic Money Philosophy, you will get the results you want—and many times, results that are so much better.

Can you stay focused? Yes. Will you need to build those muscles? Yes. Will you need to keep working them out, much like you must go to the gym to stay fit and strong? *Yes.* You can, and you must! Why?

What other option do you have? You can, of course, revert to cursing situations as they pop up, complain about any lack and limitation you're experiencing, and of course, stress out! But not one of these reactions will get you any closer to more money or a peaceful resolution. From where I sit, now that you know a better way, your best option is to give Magic Money a try, play with it until you master it, and commit to doing it for the rest of your life!

The Five Steps for Magic Money Maximization

From this point forward, when you receive any income (wages, salaries, checks, royalties, interest payments, distributions, or even cash), you will manage it with intention and purpose. You will distribute it in the way that communicates to the powers that be, namely your subconscious mind and the Universe-at-large, you are grateful to have received it and you know there is more on the way.

The way you send this message is by executing the Five Magic Money Steps:

1. Give money away.

2. Put money in savings.

3. Put money toward any debt you have.

4. If you're self-employed, put money aside for tax time.

5. Set aside money for *fun*.

For each of one through four, I suggest 10% (I'll explain why in a moment). You can test the Magic Money Philosophy by starting with 1%. The percentage you initially choose is up to you. The most important aspect of this process is your commitment to the process—this is the key to your success. Each action you take shows the Universe you are grateful for what you've received, you can be entrusted with it because you're going to be respectful of it—and of yourself. With just 1%, you can commit to the Magic Money Philosophy and enact the magic for yourself, proving it really does work.

Here's why each of the above five steps is important: respectful distribution of your money with intention and purpose is the ultimate sign of respect. It shows respect for yourself, for your money, and for your future.

As you continue to use the Magic Money Philosophy, you will notice your financial situation steadily improving. At first, you might have to scale back to distribute your income as I have suggested. It won't be long before you notice you can practice the Magic Money Philosophy, pay your bills with ease, and have plenty of money left over to do with as you please—and soon, more money will flow to you *as if by magic*.

Magic Money Step One: Give it Away

The Universe recognizes your tithe, or gift, as a sign you are grateful and want more. Giving away a portion of your income is the first step because it activates the magic. Not only does the Universe think it is fantastic you are giving away money, but also your subconscious mind takes note as well. *Gosh, if he's giving away money, that must mean we have plenty of money. Oh great! We have plenty of money. Cool. Giving away money is cool, let's get some more so we can have more, save more, and give more away!*

Learning about the act of tithing in the church was my first exposure to giving away money. Some people get stuck on what happens to the money, or what the church does with the money, and a host of other potential hang-ups.

While you can give to your church, ultimately you get to choose where the money goes as long as you follow the two cardinal rules of giving in the Magic Money Philosophy:

1. Before you do anything else with any income you receive, you give a portion away, and

2. You give it with no expectation of return.

You get to choose who gets the cash: a charity that pulls at your heartstrings, an organization doing good works, and of course, you can give it to your church, synagogue, chapel, or wherever you worship (if you do).

I advise using your gift money to make the world a better place, as a thank you to the person or institution that was the catalyst for you receiving the money, or even to anonymously make someone's dreams come true (this one is especially fun).

This act isn't supposed to be used as a loan to someone (no expectation of return, remember?), or to make yourself look good (if you give to an organization, ask that it remain anonymous). The act of giving it is purely to show your conscious and subconscious minds there is more than enough. When there's more than enough, you can share.

As a final note on giving money away, you can have no say in what happens to the money. You cannot say when or how it is spent; you give joyfully and with no strings. Why? *Because that's how you want money to come to you. Right?* Right.

Magic Money Step Two: Save Some for ... Forever

The money you place in savings will give you the ultimate peace of mind: to have more than enough money to support your lifestyle today and for as long as you live (and perhaps many generations to come). An abundance of money in saving will mean you know your needs are met. You can relax because you know there is money you can lay your hands on right when you need it. It's a great feeling to have zero stress around money and to never worry about paying your bills, feeding yourself and your family, and buying what you need *and want*—or perhaps help someone at just the right moment.

Just yesterday, I heard the coolest story! (Of course, I needed a story, so the Universe sent me one.) My friend Bob shared how his friends had started a new business recently, and they were simply all out of cash. They didn't know how to make it to the point where they were bringing in money without any additional capital.

They were just hanging out in his backyard, having an informal BBQ in what my friend describes as a humble home (which he owns outright). He was so excited to share with me

92

how he casually asked how much they needed. After they told him, they proceeded to talk about how they'd emptied their savings accounts and even borrowed a bit from their friends and families. He excused himself, went inside and wrote a check to cover what they needed and a little extra, and then presented them with the check. I think this is probably one of the coolest stories I've heard lately, but here's the best part: when he handed them the check he said, *Problem solved!*

What happened next is cooler: his friends came by a week later and gave him a one-third ownership in their business. Now keep in mind Bob didn't ask for anything, the money was a *gift*, not a loan. But his friends were so grateful; they brought him into their business. How amazing is that?

Setting aside a portion of every dollar you earn, receive, find, or manifest gives you opportunities and peace of mind. Both of which are awesome!

Magic Money Step Three: Owe Nothing!

Combining a huge financial reserve with being debt-free produces such an incredible feeling of joy and freedom. There are simply not enough words to describe how amazing it truly is. The day you realize you have more money than you need, and you don't owe a dime to anyone, for anything, is a fabulous day. Additionally, when you reach complete and total financial freedom, you will be able to capitalize on opportunities because you have both the capital to fund them and the perspective to make smart financial decisions from a place of power (not stress).

The fastest path to eliminating your debt is to use a portion of every dollar that comes to you to pay off your debt. Yes, even a small percentage will enable you to make significant progress over time.

If you have debt, the best way to eliminate it is two-fold: first, don't add any more debt to your credit lines, and second, systematically pay off the debt you do have. Perhaps not unlike racking up debt, it happens one small charge, one car repair, at a time. If you are in any debt, being hard on yourself or beating yourself up doesn't serve you in any way. You are where you are, and the situation is what it is. What you *can* do is commit to paying down your debt, all debt, no matter how big or small, until it is all gone. All of it. Gone. Forever.

Paying down your debt is sometimes limited small payments. I encourage you to stay focused and committed, even if the total amount you currently owe seems overwhelming.

As I mentioned, I made weekly, small payments to pay off my debt. This consistency and frequency was ideal for a couple of reasons. One, I got almost instant gratification by making weekly payments. I saw the balance I owed decreasing *every seven days*, which was incredibly helpful to my psyche. Two, monthly interest is charged on daily balance amounts, which meant that I was paying less interest over time by making payments more often.

Whatever percentage you have committed to give away and to save, that is the same amount you will use to pay off your debt until it is all gone. Yes, I count large purchase debt, such as vehicles and residences as debt, even though some would argue buying a home with credit can be an investment. Ask anyone who bought a home in the United States in 2006, 2007, or 2008 if that home was an actual investment! I highly suggest you rent until you can afford to buy with at least 50% down, and even then, unless you're going to live in that home for decades, and can afford repairs, maintenance, and taxes with ease, *wait*. I'll discuss this more in depth in *Magic Money Mastery*.

Magic Money Step Four: Prepare for Taxes

If you're self-employed or are receiving multiple streams of income not through an employer that automatically withholds a portion of your income for taxes, consider the following:

Save approximately 20-25% of each dollar received for taxes, and consult an experienced tax professional as soon as possible. Identifying the exact percentage to put aside will prepare you for any tax bill *and* (total bonus!) simultaneously eliminate any stress you have around taxes! (You're welcome.)

Imagine having more than enough to pay your taxes each time you have to pay them. Yup, part of the Magic Money Philosophy sets you up for success in multiple ways, not the least of which is increased happiness and next-to-zero (if not zero) stress about money. An entirely different way than most people live, for sure, but one that is not only possible but can eventually be a given for you.

If you are not self-employed, the above advice still applies *because* the Magic Money Philosophy, when practiced like the star you are, will invite and result in lots of money coming to you from multiple sources on a continuous basis (and some of those will be taxable). Still check in with your tax professional about which, if any of them, will result in a tax consequence you'll want to be prepared to handle easily.

Now that we've gotten the giving, save, debt, and tax pieces handled (whew!), let's move on the to the most magical part of magic money, my personal favorite...

Magic Money Step Five: Have Fun!

Least, but certainly not last, is to set aside or simply use the same percentage as you've chosen for giving, saving, debt and possibly taxes to use for *fun*. You can define fun however you'd like, but be sure you intentionally and purposefully use this portion of your income to do something that brings you joy and happiness.

When you use a percentage of the money you earn for total, unadulterated fun, your subconscious mind gets in on the game because there's nothing it likes more than pure fun that is mandatory.

Having a good time with your money reinforces the idea that receiving money is wonderful, and therefore you will continually receive more money.

When your subconscious money deems something as negative, it does everything to avoid more negative. If up until this point, you have associated receiving money with stress and general unhappiness (perhaps because you have large unpaid bills or debt), it won't do everything in its power to bring you more money (although that seems counter-intuitive, right?).

But when you take the consistent actions to pay down your debt, and you not only see the amount you owe decreasing, while you're simultaneously having a blast with money on a regular basis, your subconscious mind is like, *Woo hoo! Receiving money is great! Let's collude with the Universe and get more money up in here! This is AWESOME!*

So, what type of fun am I suggesting? I'll give you the answer you'd get from any lawyer when asked a question: *It depends.* Truly, my friend, what and how you spend your fun money is entirely up to you, and of course, it will depend upon how much you have.

While some of life's greatest pleasures are free, others are not (but they don't cost a lot).

I'm not hard to please, so finding the perfect piece of clothing that fits like a glove (or can be altered for the same effect) on sale gives me great pleasure. One of my favorite restaurants serves cake balls for dessert, so for a fun treat I'll visit *just for dessert*. Lots of fun, total cost: six dollars.

Other times, fun costs a little more: such as a first-class upgrade on a flight or in a hotel. A few hundred extra dollars can make the difference between an experience without pleasure, and one that truly feels decadent.

While I like the idea of saving up for some "big fun," at least initially, you want to have your fun as often as possible. Identify something you consider mind-blowingly fun, and keep your eye on your fun balance until you can spring for it.

For example, Amie, one of my Experimenters, had recently gone through a divorce and money was tight when she moved to a new city. When she started practicing the Magic Money Philosophy, almost everything was out of her budget. A total bibliophile, she doesn't even own a television—choosing instead to read every spare moment. The problem: sometimes a recommended book had a price tag she didn't feel like she could justify. She just loved that the Magic Money Philosophy now only allows for, but encourages, her to spend $13.99 on an ebook, especially because her list of "must reads" contains newly-released books occupying every "hot summer reads" list. It was no surprise to me she started receiving more and more money even as she bought more and more books! Her fun money inspired the magical combination of spending money on books she truly enjoyed reading, which enabled more and more magic money to flow to her. She keeps buying and reading more books, giving her lots of joy, which then brings her more money to buy more books!

My initial purchases with my fun money were small to the fun I can afford to have today. I had a similar experience to Amie. In the beginning, I got great joy from being able to buy my favorite Chai and wandering around

Nordstrom, admiring beautiful clothes I knew I would someday be able to purchase without a second thought. Now I am able to buy a Chai and enjoy it while my personal shopper brings me items she knows I would enjoy wearing (and almost always, she's right). I can, thankfully, purchase any of the items I love without a second thought.

Here's what I know for sure: eventually you're going to have to work hard to spend all of your fun money. You might start out with just a few dollars you stretch to experience joy, but eventually the amount of money you have to spend will be more than enough for anything you'd like to do. Think first-class vacations, a new set of wheels (you will pay for with cash), or even a new home.

Sometimes I use my fun money to make someone else's life joyful, which brings me more joy and fun than almost anything I can do for myself.

No matter how you spend your fun money, *just make sure you spend it!* Just like giving, saving, and pay off your debt, do it as soon as you can and with as much happiness as you can muster. The more you do it, the more you'll get to do it!

Remember to Respect Your Money in All Ways, Always.

A high regard for money is not solely about giving, saving, and enjoying. It's also about not using money to impress others. While it's a great idea to treat others, be sure you're doing it when your house is in order.

My dear friend Elizabeth was thrilled when I shared some of my "secret sauce" with her. And once she got into the flow of Magic Money, she wouldn't stop talking about how amazing it was. But she also started doing something I didn't advise—she wouldn't let others treat her. She would buy drinks, lunches, and dinners for her friends. But she would also buy them clothes, shoes, and even the occasional big-ticket item—which sometimes put her in the position of being uncomfortably close to zero in her bank account.

While she was having fun with her money, she wasn't respectful of it because she wasn't spending it with intention and purpose. Then she would almost run out of money, although thankfully she did not dip into her savings account. As a result, she would spend a few stressful days or a week until her next cash infusion would arrive.

The best thing you can do for your family and friends is share the Magic Money Philosophy with them. Help them to get into the flow of their own magic and abundance. Give them a copy of this book, or tell them what you're doing and invite them to join you.

As you continue with this Philosophy eventually move into *Magic Money Mastery*, you will have more money than you could ever spend. Have you ever heard, *Give a man a fish, and you feed him for a day; teach a man to fish and you feed him for a lifetime?* I can't think of a better way to feed your friends and family for their lifetime than to teach them how to get in the flow of Magic Money and stay there!

Finally, the time has come to bring the Magic Money Philosophy all together and begin your Second Magic Money Experiment. Are you ready? Let's do this!

Chapter Seven

YOUR SECOND MAGIC MONEY EXPERIMENT

'm excited as I sit down to write this chapter. It's going to be quick and easy, and I believe it's going to change your life!

The time has come for you to embark on your Second Magic Money Experiment.

I have the feeling (and enormous hope) you will be engaging in this practice for much longer than just thirty days. This experiment, just like the one in *Beginning Magic Money*, has the potential to change everything for you. There's no way for me to share with you even a glimpse of the possibilities, possible outcomes, or magic that can, and will occur. I can only say, if we knew each other, I'd be willing to bet once you start doing this experiment, the actions you take with a hint of skepticism will be the same actions that become daily habits. You, just like me, won't be able to get enough of the good stuff.

And, as a side note, nothing I'm going to ask you to do is hard, complicated, or time consuming.

To prep for your next Experiment, let's review the guidelines of the first experiment *because* they still (and will always) apply:

One. Take responsibility for your life and everything in it.

Two. Stop complaining, moaning, or bellyaching.

Three. Keep a running gratitude list.

Four. Watch for and record, your results (money, clients, goods, services, discounts, found money, etc.).

Keep engaging the magic by continuing these practices until—*until forever.* Make them daily habits you practice, along with the

Now, let's add some new actions for this next Experiment. Mark your calendar for thirty days from today, and get ready to do the following:

One. **On the very first page of your Journal write: My Master Manifestation List.**

On this page (and you'll want to save the first 3-5 pages for an on-going list), write the master list of every thing, situation, and event you want to manifest into your life, now and in the future. You set your intentions *in writing.*

Write everything you can think of right now, and of course, leave space to add more as they occur to you.

If you have an outstanding medical bill you can't quite pay today, write *I easily paid the $2,836 bill to ABC Medical Services.* Want to gain or lose some weight? Try *I now weigh 185 lbs., am in the best shape and health of my life, and feel terrific every single day.* What's that? You've been yearning to take an Alaskan cruise? Easy like Sunday morning: *I had the best time on the*

10-day Glacier Bay Alaskan cruise aboard the Norwegian Jewel. Alaska was breathtaking, and I can't believe how much I ate!

Yup, you guessed it, you write your master list as though everything on it is already done. As one of your desires comes to mind on other days, you can add them to your daily list.

Two. **Write today's date at the top of a blank page in your Journal.**

Underneath the date, write *It is so amazing that* ... and, one line at a time, write down what you want to happen today as though it has already happened. Let me share a few examples:

- Mark is respectful and cleans his room without a reminder.

- I engaged Bob Smith as a new client, I received his signed contract, and he paid in full for one year.

- My annual review was great, and I received an 18% raise and $125,000 bonus.

- The car wash was empty, and I was in and out in twenty minutes!

- My workout was amazing, and I am stronger and faster than ever!

Look at your day, see what's on your calendar, then picture the day as already done. Imagine yourself at the end of the day today, and everything went perfectly. A pitch meeting with a prospective client? They say "yes!" and are excited to work with you. Are your kids bringing home their report cards? They arrive home, with all A's, of course, and you have a celebratory dinner at their favorite restaurant. Taking your car in for the 120,000-mile checkup? Magically, it's in terrific shape and only needs a simple oil change. Expecting a signed contract or check in the mail? Yup, it arrives on (or ahead of) schedule.

It's your job to picture each item on your list as done, each activity as though it goes perfectly. You're setting your intentions *with visualization.*

Three. Speak Magic Money.

While Magic Money isn't an official language, you do need to learn the new language of magic money to attract it!

This part of your Second Magic Money Experiment is multi-faceted:

- Speak about things only as you want them to be.

- *Cancel* any words you utter that are contrary to what you want.

- Remain unmoved when you see things moving in the wrong direction, or even results you don't want.

- Remain unattached to your outcomes.

- Ask yourself the Positive Power Questions (PPQs).

- Bless everything and everyone as good.

- Remember: everything that happens is a sign of awesomeness!

- When you ask for something, always add *this or something better*.

Four. **Practice Magic Money Maximization.**

If you haven't already, decide what percentage of all monies you receive, you're going to use to practice Magic Money Maximization (insert your pre-determined percentage for x%, below).

When you receive money (i.e., the day it's officially cleared your bank account for use, or you have the cold hard cash in your hands), do the following:

- Give x% away.

- Save x%.

- Use x% to pay off your debt.

- Set aside x% for taxes.

- Put x% in your fun account. If you can, have fun *right away!*

You might be tempted to wait until tomorrow, or the weekend, or sometime later to do your distributions. Please do it *as soon as possible.* The sooner you distribute your money, the sooner the Universe will say *Aha! She's serious! My turn to act!*

Ideally, you'll start with or increase your distributions to 10% (or more!) over time. If you are in a time of struggle financially, keep in mind the tide can turn immediately and you can absolutely find yourself flush with abundance quick as a flash!

Your intentional and timely money management will serve you in at least two ways: you will feel good and full of confidence about taking control of your money, as well as set in motion magical and invisible forces to work on your behalf.

Remember, even beginning with just 1% will fully engage Magic Money and the Universe will begin working on your behalf immediately. Remember with your First Magic Money Experiment how you experienced something incredible within the first twenty-four hours? Don't be surprised when something amazing happens.

You may notice how abundant you feel. Or, you might feel a tightness in your chest. You might be skeptical. Wherever you are on the emotional money scale is perfectly normal. Follow the steps. Review them. Commit them to memory. Take the action you're inspired to take. Record your results.

Spend at least thirty days allocating your money according to the Magic Money Philosophy, and I'm sure by the end of the thirtieth day, you will be hooked!

Chapter Eight

MORE MAGIC MONEY MASTERY

The combination of the inner work of the first Experiment with outer actions in your second Experiment is truly magical. Your mind, your lips and your feet are all moving in the same direction, and I promise you the results will astound and amaze you. I've been practicing Magic Money for two decades, and there is not one day that goes by I don't smile to myself as yet another perfectly timed result or unexpected check or new revenue stream comes into my life.

I'm just as delighted today when something magical happens as I was when I first started my Magic Money practice. There have been times when a fat chunk of money has shown up, and not a day or two later I've had an unexpected expense. I still marvel at receiving unexpected money I can use to cover an expense I wasn't expecting. And, of course, there's enough to cover the other aspects of maximization.

I'm sure you're wondering, *Will this really all work, just like that?* Yes, and no. Life isn't perfect, and neither is Magic Money. Just like any other program you begin, it takes a while to get the hang of it. You might not feel the momentum, or achieve a sense of mental peace for a time. You will have unexpected expenses, and you may have to dip into your savings to cover them. But I promise you this: the more you practice all aspects of Magic Money, the better you'll get.

You will see you much to be grateful for, and you will have less to complain about. You'll have more money in reserve. You'll be able to meet challenges with a positive attitude, and capitalize on opportunities because you have money in reserve. You will have fun with money, and money will become fun for you.

Remember this: setbacks are not a valid reason to quit. Come right back to your Magic Money practices, even if you drain your savings account. The next time you receive any income, put your next deposit into your savings account.

Keep in mind you've been handling money in non-Magic Money fashion for years! How long? Five years? Thirty years? It takes a few weeks for the effects of a new diet to really kick in; it similarly takes a bit of time for Magic Money practices to stick and show results. Just like anything else, the longer you practice, the better results you will get.

And, if for any reason, you get off track—life happens, don't I know it—start again at the beginning. Re-read *Beginning Magic Money*, break out a new journal, and start a fresh thirty-day experiment. It might just take more than one "go" for Magic Money to become habitual.

Flash Forward

There will come a time you will marvel at the money you have in reserve. You won't believe the daily balance in your checking account because it's gonna be big! You will notice less stress in your neck and shoulders. You will be more

117

happy, relaxed, and playful. And, you have love picking up the check *because you can.*

A year from now, you should have a nice nest egg, a long list of manifestations, perhaps an even longer list of things you want to manifest, and (my favorite) a long list of fun memories to look back on. You will be living a life of true financial freedom and independence.

Ten years from now, you will have more than enough on hand and in reserve to live the rest of your life in any manner you choose.

But Wait! There's More!

I originally planned just two books in the series; then I realized there are several additional practices I engage in to keep the magic flowing. If you are having fun and want more, you'll love *Magic Money Mastery.*

I know this isn't "breaking news," but Magic Money isn't just about the money. My philosophy includes the ability to have an abundance of everything you need to live a happy, productive life—which obviously includes money.

When you've completed thirty days of your Second Magic Money Experiment, you're ready for what's next: *Magic Money Mastery.* In the third and final installment in this series, I don't just pull back the curtain—I tear it down! I share everything I do to earn, save, share, grow, and multiply every aspect of my abundance.

I look forward to seeing you there!

I wish you a life of Magic Money!

GRATITUDE

A huge bucket of thanks to my Experimenters and Magic Money Practitioners! Thank you for validating my process. Wishing you a lifetime of magic money and abundance of every wonderful thing!

WHO IS HOLLY

Holly Alexander is the author of the three-book series: *Magic Money:* A Course in Creating Abundance. She's a serial entrepreneur, multiple-business owner, philanthropist, wife, mom, avid traveler, reader, and explorer.

She believes you can have, do, and be everything you want to have, do, and be when you treat life and money with the respect they deserve. You can find out more at MagicMoneyBooks.com.

Made in United States
Troutdale, OR
03/12/2024

18377930R10076